CENTERED *Self*, CENTERED *Horse*

A SIMPLE GUIDE TO HORSEMANSHIP

AIR
Awareness In Riding

Published by Awareness In Riding
Awareness In Riding, 9946 North Clear Lake Road, Milton, Wisconsin 53563,
U.S.A.

First Edition
1 2 3 4 5 6 7 8 9 10

Library of Congress Control Number 2008200357
ISBN 978-0-9814949-0-6

Book Design by Erica K. Frei

BOOKS ARE AVAILABLE AT QUANTITY DISCOUNTS WHEN USED TO PROMOTE PROD-
UCTS OR SERVICES. FOR INFORMATION PLEASE WRITE TO AWARENESS IN RIDING,
9946 NORTH CLEAR LAKE ROAD, MILTON, WISCONSIN 53563.

AWARENESS IN RIDING

EDICATION

The long history of this book would likewise garner a long dedication. To all of the people I have ever met, and all of the horses I have had the pleasure of working with, without which I would find myself standing in a different place.

¶ To my mother; who has never given up on me, and has always told me that chasing my dreams is worthwhile.

¶ To my dad; whose silent support has given me the example and encouragement to continue on no matter how much I would have liked to give up in times of difficulty.

¶ To my friend, mentor and colleague Tracy; who passed along her never-ending patience in regard to the horse, a lesson of unending value.

¶ To my friend Jason; who never allowed an excuse for failure, never questioned my ability to pursue my passion, and has always encouraged me to be myself.

ACKNOWLEDGEMENTS

To the many Starbucks and libraries that have allowed me unlimited access to their chairs and electricity. Thanks to my parents for their undying support. My horses for their willingness over the years to participate as Guinea Pigs.

All of the teachers past, present and future, who knowingly and unknowingly passed along small kernels of truth. This chickadee appreciates the nourishment.

NTRODUCTION

This book, written with every ounce of my present understanding, has been a long time in coming. I have worked with horses since I was 9 years old, and the road to where I stand with this work of literature has not always been the smooth one that I may have dreamed of when just starting out. I don't believe that I am alone in this, and that is precisely why I have been compelled to write.

From the outside, I have been told I have a natural talent when it comes to working with horses. Over the course of my riding career, I have inspired many horses to perform a variety of tasks, from the simple to the seemingly complex. I have crossed over into many different disciplines and found success equally. I have encouraged stallions to behave like geldings, and geldings to reserve a sense of stallion-hood in their actions.

This assumption may be easy to jump to, but vastly incorrect. I have struggled learning the very basics, and my misunderstandings have at times gone on longer than necessary due to my pride holding me back from asking for clarity or admitting I did not understand.

I have fallen off my fair share of horses, untrained well trained horses and incorrectly trained others that I started myself. While I could choose to dwell on the failures I have faced, instead I have chosen to reflect and learn as much as possible from each situation.

All that I have learned has culminated into more of a life-style, than a career style. I have learned that there is no separating the way I treat my horses from the way I treat other people. When I am stressed in one area of my life, it will have an impact on my riding. Likewise, when I am happy, confident, and relatively carefree my horses show me the same in return.

This book is many things; an introduction to equitation, a guide to developing yourself as a rider, and a summation of where equitation peaks. It was not written in the pursuit of an "a + b = c" type of manual. Instead, it is a guide to being a great rider, trainer, and handler. Changing the way in which you approach the horse for training directly influences your actions and the outcome.

A large issue addressed in this book is that of resistance, and the very creation of this book required that I stop employing force in my attempts to convey my thoughts. Over the course of the last 10 years, I have written enough material for around twenty books, however none of them were what I really wanted to or had to say, and instead of allowing myself to be guided to writing what I wanted, I attempted to force the words onto paper.

Once I stopped forcing, there was no resistance to my words, and this book literally wrote itself in less than a week. Though it may be small, it is deep, and I hope that you read it continuously, to discover all of the nuances that one can only find as they continue to rediscover and develop themselves.

What I am is never as important as what I do. The actions I make, the words I say, the motivation behind my riding. I can be famous and abuse my horses in private, or be virtually unknown and manage the most brilliant and kind horse skills. I can be old and ignorant, or young and intelligent. This book is for those who are ready to reach for what they want out of themselves as riders by setting aside their preconceived notions of ability.

Enjoy!

> "WHATEVER COURSE YOU DECIDE UPON, THERE IS ALWAYS SOMEONE TO TELL YOU THAT YOU ARE WRONG. THERE ARE ALWAYS DIFFICULTIES ARISING WHICH TEMPT YOU TO BELIEVE THAT YOUR CRITICS ARE RIGHT. TO MAP OUT A COURSE OF ACTION AND FOLLOW IT TO AN END REQUIRES COURAGE."
>
> **RALPH WALDO EMERSON**

CENTERED *Self*, CENTERED *Horse*

A SIMPLE GUIDE TO HORSEMANSHIP

CONTENTS

To know oneself is to know, appreciate, love, and care about all of your surroundings and the beings within them. To know more of the commonalities between one another, and little of the differences. To see yourself in their eyes, before you know their eyes are not a part of yourself.

EFINITION

In order to utilize the contents of a book, an idea, a theory, a concept, it is important to have an understanding of the mind behind it.

To me, the whole of horsemanship, equitation, riding, training, and generally interacting with the horse can be summed up to an extent as being 'balance in movement.' Or, dynamic balance. This balance could be balance in movement of the mind, of the body, of thoughts, actions, feelings, emotions, etc. Balance in movement of life.

The horse himself is not even the end goal in our pursuit of riding, but rather acts as a barometer, showing more clearly the results of our ability of dynamic balance. He mirrors our emotional, spiritual, mental, and physical state. He gives us instant feedback as to our level of understanding, compassion, attention, patience, etc. The actions of the horse can often become the goal in the mind of the rider, when it is so much more, and so much less.

So, in that regard, horsemanship to me is merely a tool of insight in finding the peace, happiness and passion of life.

Harmony exists only when all of the elements involved in it's creation are balanced and equal. Equal skill, tact, balance, speed, direction, weight, pressure, etc. When any of these elements is not equal or in balance, harmony does not exist. This is why harmony is difficult and so cherished, because we must learn to become jugglers and masters of all trades.

ARMONIZING THE HORSE

However we wish to define it; horsemanship, equitation, riding, training, and handling are all one in the same. They are intertwined closely with every other area of our life. We may try to separate and sort out horsemanship into different categories, by experience, discipline, breed, gender, even by what trainer's philosophies you follow. In the end they are all the same, all connected in one way or another.

> **THOUGH WE TRY TO COMPARTMENTALIZE, WE CANNOT SEPARATE OURSELVES FROM ONE ANOTHER.**

It is not that all disciplines or approaches are identical, that is obvious by the differences in tack and equipment, lingo, and theories. These details are small however, mere blades of grass in the midst of a vast forest. What is the same is the underlying cause behind them all. In everything we do with the horse, we are drawn towards harmony. We may not realize it, we might think that our motivation is driven by sheer love for the horse, excitement over extreme jumps, simple companionship, or perhaps the accolades earned from successful competition or breeding programs. All of these and more involve some form of harmony. It does not matter if we attempt to gain this harmony in English, Western, Dressage, Eventing, or simply riding for the joy of it; it is harmony all the same. From the outside they may all appear to be very different elements, but if we step back to see the larger picture it becomes more apparent to see the ties that bind them all together. This harmony is not restricted solely to the horse's performance either. Riders who harmonize well with their horse's movement and with their use of the aids are often termed elegant or naturally talented riders.

Harmony is made up of many components, and it is the equal development of these components that leads us all the closer to achieving harmony. To have one without the other leaves something to be desired. Harmony is also the willingness to be led, to follow along the unrestricted path or the path of least resistance. This is the vital element, that to harmonize comes without force or resistance.

BEAUTY LIES IN THE SIMPLICITY REQUIRED TO DO WHAT OUGHT TO BE COMPLICATED AND COMPLEX BUT APPEARS EFFORTLESSLY PERFORMED.

THAT IS THE ART.

Harmony, a noun.

1. AGREEMENT OR ACCORD
2. A PLEASING COMBINATION OF ELEMENTS, OR ARRANGE-
MENT OF SOUNDS.
3. (MUSIC) THE ACADEMIC STUDY OF CHORDS
4. (MUSIC) TWO OR MORE NOTES PLAYED SIMULTANEOUSLY
TO PRODUCE A CHORD
5. (MUSIC) THE RELATIONSHIP BETWEEN TWO DISTINCT
MUSICAL PITCHES (MUSICAL PITCHES BEING FREQUENCIES OF
VIBRATION WHICH PRODUCE AUDIBLE SOUND) PLAYED SIMUL-
TANEOUSLY

While harmony is often considered in the way of music, there is a harmony present in every action that we take. For example, if we replace the chords of music with the actions of our aids we can work to harmonize each action with one another. Thus producing a more pleasing movement or response from the horse.

The ability to harmonize ourselves with the horse is akin to harmonizing ourselves with all of the surroundings in our life. It is an eternal learning lesson. We take in feedback and adjust accordingly. This is the development of harmony.

NOTES

NOTES

That which is done for a reward but requires overcoming pain is less rewarding than doing something that is in itself the reward.

$\mathcal{P}$AINFUL HORSE

The horse is, at its most elementary level, an extension of ourselves. That is not a statement made in arrogance, rather an observation of what is. It is for this reason that we must be especially vigilant in our care of any pain that may arise through the riding and training of him.

The horse can display issues of pain for any number of reasons, and outside of an obvious injury or improperly fitting tack, we must also be aware of the emotional and mental pain that can manifest itself in a physical form.

> **PAIN DOES NOT SUPPORT LEARNING. LEARNING DOES NOT RELY UPON PAIN.**

Resistance is a type of mental distress which manifests itself directly in the physical form. Muscles contract, movement becomes hesitant, stilted, and so on. Emotional pain can also manifest in a physical form, through muscle quivering and spasms, hyper-sensitivity to touch or signals, and erratic responses.

It is always in our interest to be conscious of the horse's signs of pain or distress. Any distress of an emotional or mental cause, will eventually show itself in the horse's physicality, and can be a direct cause of injury, infection, disease, and premature death in the horse, not to mention directly affecting the horse's performance.

It is important that we reduce the number of chronic stressers found in the horse's environment as they can be direct contributors to health problems including osteoporosis, reduced immune function, impaired mental functions, and irreparable cell damage. Some chronic stressers can include stabling in stalls, physical isolation, herd hostility and aggression, inconsistencies in handling and training.

Every effort should be made to eliminate stresses that cause habitual vices such as pawing, weaving, windsucking, cribbing, self-inflicted injury, ulcers, aggression, and depression. These vices not only serve to drain the horse's energy and vitality, but put humans at risk with every encounter. Much like you avoid the man who is over-stressed at work for fear that the next straw will break the camel's back and he might bring a gun to work to 'vent' his stress, the horse too has a breaking point that can be extremely dangerous.

Stress caused directly by the training and riding practices employed are also important to become conscious of. This stress manifests itself in resistance and responses which do not have a sliding scale. When the horse explodes, spooks violently, etc. The horse can also shows the opposite, by shutting down or appearing dull or lazy. The horse which is devoid of chronic stress and has a confident and trusting relationship with humans gives responses which follow upon a sliding scale of consistency.

Pain responses that appear to come from the tack, are often caused by the rider's lack of tact, finesse, and lightness in the aids, particularly in the case of bits. The best fitting saddle will pain the horse's back if the rider sitting upon it lacks balance, independence of the aids, and harmony with the horse's movement.

A rider who lacks balance will likewise always ride a horse which has compromised balance. Over time, imbalance leads to injury on some level, if not several, leading to pain or dysfunction in the gaits. The horse often learns how to compensate for the rider's lack of balance, but this compensation is not a desired solution, like a band-aid on the severed artery, so to speak.

Imbalances in the horse's gaits, faltered steps in movements and maneuvers, problems transitioning in gaits, are in most cases rider error. There will be exceptions to this rule, and a true underlying physical problem should always be evaluated for by a veterinarian.

The horse will act as our body, with us being the mind. The body will show the dysfunction in the mind, the horse shows our own errors through the ones he performs beneath us. Uneven tracking in the gaits, balance issues when maneuvering, transitions that are either lethargic or rushed, etc., can also stem from mental or emotional causes. Pain emanating from an emotional level; that of fears, anxiety, panic, depression, excitement, etc., are solved only through establishing calm trust. A healthy horse is never sensitive or dull, they are all equally curious, excitable, calm, and obedient to the aids. A healthy horse that is, who is handled by a healthy rider.

In the case of a horse who has muscle memory pain, the horse who continues to display imbalances or 'pain' without cause aside from previous handling, will take time more than remedy. Our actions in this case must never support the horse's fears, but they must be calm and clear actions which serve to disarm the horse's resistance and self-protecting actions.

The use of gimmicks and training 'aids' such as draw reins, tie-downs, and specialized lunge equipment, only serves to take away the horse's ability to communicate to us our areas of weakness, excessive force, or imbalance. They do damage to both horse and rider. If we were to take all of these options away, all that would be left to train the horse is time, patience, compassion, and observational skills. The reliance on the mind vs. equipment causes us to trade in muscular strength and force for the power of our mind and to become more dependent upon developing the horse's own intelligence in the relationship. The truth is, that we are all perfectly equipped to handle, ride, and train our horses to the highest levels possible. The use of expensive or specialized equipment is not the key to horsemanship. What we cannot purchase is our mind, through which all natural or unnatural skill must first be rendered before we can apply it with the horse.

Any piece of equipment has the potential to be mild or severe, harmless or injurious. It is all in our intention, skill and intelligent use. Only the most skilled have the tact to utilize the oft-promoted gimmicks and gadgets, and it is those same persons who do not need to utilize these tools, eliminating their purpose altogether.

The most powerful evidence of skilled riding and the lack of pain or resistance, is relinquishing the control of the horse's body to himself, and keeping only the subtle influence of weight and aids to direct the horse to our desires.

> PROBLEMS ARE NOT SOLVED BY EXAMINING THE SYMPTOMS ALONE.
>
> PROBLEMS ARE SOLVED BY DISCOVERING AND EXAMINING THE CAUSE.

NOTES

NOTES

We have the power to increase or decrease our understanding of pain at any moment. That is the power of pain, that it lies within our ultimate control. We can focus on it, or we can distract ourselves. We wield a power of mind that may be unavailable to the horse. We do not depend on the thought that the horse will forget his pain like we can, and in turn we search out solutions to our pain, just as we do for our horse.

PAINFUL SELF

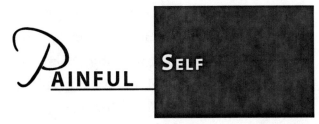

Our view of pain in regards to our horse is often reflected by the way we view our own pain. We all experience pain on the level of physical, mental, and emotional whether great or small, whether we are conscious or unconscious of it. When we suppress or ignore our own pain, it is difficult not to do likewise with the horse. We lose our compassion in regards to his pain. It becomes easy to say the horse does not experience emotional pain, when we ourselves are unaware of the impact the repression of our own emotional pain is having in our life.

Pain is always a signal, a warning, feedback. Pain tells us when we are on the path to injury or when we've arrived. When we ignore this pain, on whatever level, it only builds and leads to further damage. Our suppression of pain not only magnifies in our own life, it spills over to the horses and people we interact with as well.

Physical pain holds us back from giving trust to the horse in situations we view potentially injurious. Emotional pain can prevent us from giving the horse boundaries, or cause us to 'make friends' when it is inappropriate. Mental pain can keep us from seeking out help when we are confused, frustrated, or disillusioned with our horse. Overall, pain is a sign that things are not working, there is a link in our chain that is rusting, twisted, or broken. Perhaps there are not enough links in the chain, or too many. Often it is the areas we believe cannot have an impact on our pain that are most influential, no matter how seemingly insignificant. Like our horse, if we hope to perform at our greatest potential, we have to take care of ourselves in every possible area.

It is through the resistance of our pain, that it endures all the longer. It hinders because we fight it. We avoid discovering the cause and settle only on finding a cure. Before we can cure the pains we experience, we must find the cause, the true cause. To attempt the cure of the symptoms only creates stress and compensational responses in other areas.

It can certainly be frightening to think of embracing our pains, or moving closer into them. To stop resisting and allow them to be. Fears begin to fester in our mind. The 'what if's, all of the thoughts of what could happen if we do not fight against or attempt to hide or downplay the influence of pain in our lives. The simple truth is that if we are alive, we will experience pain at some point in our life, on some level. We all experience pain and it is hardly something to feel the need to hide.

When we move into feeling our feelings fully, we set ourselves free. The only power they have is through stifling our action, our living, our life. When we continue to live that pain loses its power.

The ability to feel feelings fully, is in part due to developing our ability to describe specifically what those feelings are. When we are specific with what we are feeling, they become honest, they become worth feeling.

It is the murky, muddy feelings that keep us up the river without a paddle. For example, using words like; fine, okay, kinda, sometimes, etc., are not specific. They are words we habitually use in describing the way we feel so we don't have to be specific. They are avoiding words.

Specific words are definable. When used they convey a widespread understanding of exactly what it is you are feeling. Basically, if you can describe your feelings in a way that everyone in the room can understand then you are feeling them fully. You are being specific, there is no room for your own misunderstanding of your feelings.

When we work to be specific with our horses, we start with ourselves. When we work to be specific in conveying instruction or teaching, we start with ourselves and our horses. This is the foundation for our strength, that of honesty to ourselves.

NOTES

NOTES

We are all things in our life, we are weak and strong, we are old and young, we are smart and slow. We are at times any of these things in our life. Because we are these things, we learn to be sympathetic, compassionate, tender, and tolerant with they who are also travelling these paths - be they horse or human.

$\mathcal{S}$EPARATION vs. COMPASSION

Separation is all too prevalent in everything we do with the horse. We separate ourselves based on the tack we use, the discipline we ride in, the level we ride at, the breed of horse, or the stable we ride at. We even separate ourselves from our horses, failing to see ourselves in them. The use of compassion in riding and training is all too important, because it is what gives us the insight to see that we are using too much pressure, or asking the horse to perform something that he is not yet ready for and more.

Compassion is a lack of separation, our ability to see ourselves as the other person, as being the same. It also applies to the way in which we view our horse. Compassion allows us to think about how we would like to be treated or how we would feel in that situation. Certainly, we can be overly compassionate when we fail to see that both the horse and ourselves still need boundaries, direction and discipline at times.

Compassion is *not* pity. Pity serves little purpose but to stroke the ego. Compassion plays a role of change. Pity plays a role of stagnation and the replaying of things we cannot change.

For the horse who is being kicked continuously in a failed attempt to elicit forward movement, compassion allows you to see how you would feel if someone was continuously jabbing at your ribs in an effort to have you dance with them. For the horse the most logical response is to buck. Compassion can also be a difficult emotion to have at times. There have been more than enough occasions when I have had to dismiss myself from the bleachers at a show, unable to hold back the tears as I witnessed all of the force and abuse being used. Now I remember to bring a box of Kleenex and my own compassion for company.

> IT IS WHEN OUR ENERGY IS ALLOWED TO GROW TO OVERFLOWING THAT WE FIND COMPASSION. IT SIMPLY POURS FROM US AS A CUP OVERFULL.

With compassion, we can recognize when we have gone too far, or are on the edge. Compassion is what keeps us from abusing our horse, from neglecting him. It is often what compels us to care for him, because we know how we would like to be cared for. It is that vital element in training, that when absent leaves the door open to using any means to achieve our goal.

Compassion is in part our way to give to the community, to think of more than ourselves in the greater scheme. An essential component to our relationship with the horse. When we think about more than ourselves we include not only the horse we are working with, but everyone we interact with.

EVERY ACTION WE MAKE, EVERY WORD WE SPEAK AND EVERY THOUGHT WE THINK, AFFECTS MORE THAN JUST OURSELVES.

WE RADIATE THE ENERGY WE CREATE THROUGH THESE THINGS TO EVERYONE AND EVERYTHING WE COME INTO CONTACT WITH. WE ARE ALL CONNECTED.

NOTES

NOTES

"Do not believe in anything simply because you have heard it. Do not believe in anything simply because it is spoken and rumored by many. Do not believe in anything simply because it is found written in your religious books. Do not believe in anything merely on the authority of your teachers and elders. Do not believe in traditions because they have been handed down for many generations. But after observation and analysis, when you find that anything agrees with reason and is conducive to the good and benefit of one and all, then accept it and live up to it."

Guatama Siddharta (Buddha)

UN-MECHANIZING THE HORSE

From desiring harmony, we've fallen into the habit of approaching the horse in a way that is more consistent with directing a vehicle. We've learned to treat him like a stiff, unyielding, unthinking inanimate object. Somewhere in our subconscious we are trained to believe that the beauty and energy of the horse can be contained and controlled utilizing force and mechanics. We have been led to believe that they can be installed with push buttons and specific controllers. This works only if we then dismiss the validity of the horse as a thinking, feeling creature.

BELLS AND WHISTLES DO NOT COME INSTALLED...

The horse's intelligence and sensitivity goes without saying, and it is because of this that he can often take on qualities that may remind us of that mechanized object we pretend we are riding around. The same can be said of ourselves as well, there are times when we may have learned that the best way to approach life is with a no questions asked attitude, simply obeying the orders of our boss, significant other, family, friends, or social rules. When we live in this way, just like the horses functioning on this plane, we rarely experience happiness or the pursuit of our passion. The mechanized thought goes against all that we wish to develop and create in the horse. If we wish to retain his beauty we have to discover what qualities go into the making of that beauty and give them back to the horse in our requests. If we wish to retain his natural energy, we have to discover the qualities that his energy contains. What we are unwilling or unable to give to the horse we cannot expect in return.

Fluidity is borne out of slow, deliberate movement. Avoiding the mechanical trap is likewise borne out of slow, deliberate movement. This movement can be defined as both mental and physical, it exists in the physical plane, but its existence can be changed based on the mental perception of it.

When we are unfamiliar with the movement, it will naturally be perceived as fast; it is out of our ability to follow the movement and influence it intentionally. When we become familiar with a movement, its once perceived excessive speed and lack of control now becomes slow to our perception and easy to manipulate. Then we find ourselves moving faster than necessary, so we must practice slowing the movement that has been perfected at speed.

Our mental interpretation directly affects the influence we

have over the fluidity of the movement. When we are dealing with an inanimate object which presents no danger to us physically, it is not a dangerous thing to 'practice' refining our movement or influence at a speed that is out of our control. Over time we will eventually come to equalize our perception and gain influence. When we are dealing with either an inanimate object that can cause us harm, or another living being, it serves both us and the other person or animal better to move only slightly into the area of speed, finding fluidity in stages.

> TRAINING A YOUNG HORSE IS SIMPLE, BECAUSE THERE IS NO UN-TRAINING INVOLVED. TRAINING A YOUNG HORSE IS ALSO DIFFICULT BECAUSE HE HAS ALL OF HIS CURIOSITY, SENSITIVITY, INTELLIGENCE, AND UNRESTRICTED ENERGY THAT A TRAINED HORSE OFTEN HAS LESS OF OR HAS BEEN PERVERTED WITH TRAINING.

Movement created out of fear, anxiety, pain or threat of injury is neither harmonious nor the sign of a relationship. We are capable of such deep communication with the horse as to request the subtlest and most physically and emotionally demanding responses with merely a word, phrase, or small movement.

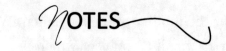

NOTES

NOTES

Listening, not talking, is perhaps the most caring thing we can do for one another. A well tuned ear and silent listener are far more effective than even the best intentioned of words. Who does not wish to be heard, including the horse, for they are few and far between if anything more than a myth.

QUALITY OF TOUCH

In the un-mechanizing of the horse, we also train ourselves to move without mechanic reflexes. We become the dancer, the swimmer, the painter. We develop the creator inside each of us, because horsemanship truly is an art. Just as any endeavor can be taken to the level of art, it is through our self reflection and discovery that we find the artistic rider inside each of us. When we work the horse in this place everything becomes fluid and simple.

> OUR ONLY REWARD IS IN THE ACTION ITSELF, NOT THE POTENTIAL RESULT. WHEN OUR ACTIONS ARE JOYOUS AND ENJOYABLE, SO WILL THE RESULTS BE.

Quality of touch refers to more than the use of our hands. Although the rein aids are a primary source of communication with the horse, the energy that feeds this quality has to come from our very being. Our whole body conveys this quality and it becomes apparent with the use of our aids; visual, vocal, and kinesthetic.

The way in which we best control the intent of our touch is through a present mind. Letting go of the thoughts about the future, and releasing our responsibility of the past. The only time that we can influence directly is the here and now. When we allow ourselves to live in the future, we are asleep. When we base our actions on thought that is stuck in the past, we become dead.

If our hope is for the horse to become attentive to our actions, and be present in the moment, we must first lead the way. We must put all of our mental, physical, and emotional energy into the split second which is occurring at this very moment.

It is difficult to turn off the thoughts which lead to future and past, because they are normally a constant hum in the mind. They fill in the otherwise 'uncomfortable silences' that would leave room for listening to what is being experienced by our senses. They are a convenient distraction which does not run out of fuel. It is often a safety blanket. What do we focus on if we do not think of our future? How do we move past our past if we do not think about what occurred in it?

To hold to us a specific goal we wish to find in our future, and then let it go. To remember something poignant in our past for a brief moment and then let it go. That is what serves us. But when we run the historical newscast or the announcements of what it is that we are pursuing 24/7, they lose their meaning. They become ordinary, everyday inescapable experiences.

The horse too will begin to wonder, 'why should I pay attention when my rider is off in la la land?' In our lack of a present mind, we miss the subtle nuances that occur in those moments of present. We miss them, and as a result our actions are delayed, hurried, and less coordinated. We fail to harmonize with the horse because the sound track we are listening to is playing out of sync.

TOUCH IS FIRST FINDING CONTACT, THEN RELEASING IT UNTIL IT IS NEARLY LOST. INITIALLY, THIS QUALITY OF TOUCH WILL FEEL LIKE THERE IS NOTHING THERE, THAT YOU HAVE NO CONTROL. THE SECOND ACT OF TOUCH INVOLVES LISTENING. WHEN YOU ARE AT THE STAGE OF TOUCH THAT YOU FEEL NOTHING, THEN YOU BEGIN TO LISTEN.

OVER TIME THAT SILENCE TURNS INTO A GREAT WAVE OF NOISE THAT YOU WILL WONDER YOU COULD HAVE MISSED BEFORE.

BE CAREFUL NOT TO SKIP THE STEP OF LISTENING. LISTENING GIVES YOU MORE INFORMATION THAN ACTION EVER COULD.

NOTES

NOTES

Art is the culmination of each part involved, that is what makes the art. The piece itself would not be art if it were only based on the end result - that is manufacturing. It is not beauty to hold a piece of machined 'art,' it is in the energy, love, and discipline involved in making the art that gives it power. Riding is the same - the culmination of all the ingredients. The beauty lies in the individual parts working together to create the art.

The Artist

Just like any artistic endeavor, our individual refinement can prove taxing. To say that every rider is capable of it is no lie, however more accurate is that not every rider is willing to put in the time, energy, and mental commitment to achieve it. More than the pure refinement is the energy behind it, the intention. Passion and general interest are separated at this junction.

Being a creator, and allowing creativity to occur can leave a person feeling vulnerable at times because we put all of ourselves into that creation, the art. We are not holding back, and as a result we are not left protecting any part of ourselves from criticism or judgment. When a person in this position does meet opposition to their art, they can feel shut down, angry, or afraid of attempting it again. It is this experience that feeds our ability to grow, change, and learn; giving us the chance to become the best at what we love – working with horses.

When our horse is given criticism or redirected because he did not perform as we requested, we expect that he try again without complaint. Our ability to return this favor to the horse is what our relationship is all about, give and take. We are willing to be made vulnerable, in the same way we make our horse vulnerable.

Our ego will feel injured certainly, because it is always striving to be better than, have more, mean more, be more attractive, etc. When it is told otherwise, feelings of anger, resentment, the need to compete, put down, argue, etc., will come to the surface. When the ego is not functioning, criticism does not feel personal, and it is taken merely as it was given, with the intent of assisting in growth and learning.

It is important that as riders, we ride for the sake of riding. To get distracted into competition or goals that we parade around as though banners on a flag, are only for the purpose of soothing our ego. They have no real purpose outside of that. Goals which cause us to reach deeper into ourselves, learn, gain consciousness and self-awareness, are the goals that riders are best to pursue. They are goals that when achieved will mean little to anyone outside of yourself but will shine bright and attract like minds to you.

The horse cares little about ribbons, competitions, or other public achievements. The horse's greatest desire comes down to having the feeling of safety, a trustworthy relationship with his human, and to have clear signals about what is expected, requested and desired from him. His needs are simple.

The rider's desires become complicated, only from the ego. Without the ego, the rider's desires remain simple: to have a relationship with the horse that is safe (relatively), confident, harmonious, trustworthy, and clear. When those criteria are met, any and every movement, maneuver, gait, air of fantasy, and level of riding is easily achieved.

NOTES

NOTES

There are things that cannot be described; a feel, a look, a touch. These things have to be discovered, they are what creates tact. They are what creates harmony. They are what is worked for, but often missed.

$\mathcal{T}$ACT & FLUIDITY

In this pursuit of art, we have to learn to develop our tact and fluidity. The potential skill and sensitivity available in the hands is oft-underestimated. It is said that a trained massage therapist can detect as little as half a degree of temperature change with their fingertips. Even without the skills of a trained massage therapist, our hands are immense resources for retrieving information about the horse. Not only do we have highly developed sensitivity in our fingers, we are also accustomed to using our hands for the vast majority of our tasks.

Tact and fluidity are a result of developing a sort of sliding scale with your aids. Initially, getting from point A to point B may result in 3 steps; our ultimate goal is to develop thousands if not millions of steps between every point A and B. Just as a movie with more frames per second will appear more fluid, our actions will also take on a fluid feel the more steps we take between movements. The few short steps we take in picking up our reins or giving a leg aid can be lengthened to seemingly ridiculous lengths with the possible addition of innumerable steps. While we certainly don't want to take all day to pick up the reins, there is always the possibility of it when working horses that need more steps, more fluidity. We never discount or dismiss the benefits that this can have in riding and training.

If we want fluidity from our horse, we have to give it in response. We must be willing to take the time to develop our fluidity, in particular when it is unnatural for us. On flights I have likely garnered some odd looks as I worked for hours at a time to complete my circle-a-words using my left hand, which is not my dominant hand. Of course the results looked like I had some sort of neurological deterioration, combined with rage as there were holes in the pages from my inability to regulate the pressure appropriately. For me, it is important to have the use of my hands as equally skilled and tactful as possible, and I practice it in ways that may not be directly related to the horse.

When we take this concept of time, patience, practice, and unlimited possibilities, we set the stage for the horse. Our energy creates something more vibrant than is capable when we work with the mind-set of not enough time, being rushed and impatient. Like the horse who is impossible to catch when you have only five minutes vs. the horse who is a breeze when you have all day - our horses are intuitive to all of the energy we emit. It all starts in our mind.

There are always an infinite number of steps we can make between actions, movements and maneuvers. We are only limited by our imagination and patience. When we work in a manner that takes a long period of time we develop our ability to see the smallest of details. Details that otherwise do not exist in our consciousness when we work at faster speeds.

Over time, the development of our awareness becomes automatic, second nature, and our ability to be as skilled while moving quickly increases. Nothing done poorly at a slow speed ever improves at faster speeds. The speed may simply mask the obviousness of the errors.

WE PRACTICE, NOT *FOR* THE PERFECTION. WE PRACTICE AS A MEANS OF INVITING THE PERFECTION WE DESIRE. OUR INTENTION IS THE INVITATION, BECAUSE THERE MAY BE A KEY TO LEARNING THAT INVOLVED A DETOUR FROM PERFECTION TO ACHIEVE. WE DO NOT PRACTICE THE PERFECTION AT EVERY STEP, WE PRACTICE THE AWARENESS TO KNOW WHAT DIRECTION PERFECTION LIES.

NOTES

NOTES

"We do not grow absolutely, chronologically. We grow some-times in one dimension, and not in another; unevenly. We grow partially. We are relative. We are mature in one realm, childish in another. The past, present, and future mingle and pull us backward, forward, or fix us in the present. We are made up of layers, cells, constellations."

Anais Nin

Relative Pressure

Pressure is a broad term that I use to describe most if not all of our interactions with the horse. When we are within sight, we are applying pressure. When we lead him up from the pasture we apply pressure. When we lunge, ride, or drive the horse we are using pressure. There is no interaction with the horse that is not subject to pressure of some form.

> **WE DO NOT SEEK CONFORMITY WITH THE HORSE. WE SEEK TO FIND UNDERSTANDING OF WHO HE IS. WE SEEK TO UNDERSTAND HIS LIMITATIONS, TO FIND WHAT CAUSES HIM GREAT JOY AND EXCITEMENT.**

We live in a world of physical, mental and emotional pressure, without which we lack a motivator for living our life. We cannot think that all pressure is bad, because the vital job of pressure is to cause change. Bad pressure is when it is used no longer to influence change, but to force change. The only pressure we can be responsible for is that which we are applying. We must avoid absorbing, or forcing the absorption of pressure we are given or giving. This absorption proves only to begin the breakdown of communication.

Our responsibility in regards to pressure is that of observing and asking for feedback about the amount of pressure; if it is too much, too little or correct. With people this is simple, we can simply ask verbally. With the horse, we learn to receive this feedback and ask questions without the use of our voice, words have little honest meaning here. Like a mute, we must learn to rely on our other senses, in particular our eyes and touch. We learn to see the horse's emotions on a visual level, and we learn to understand pressure through our body.

We take our time, this is how we regulate our pressure. It is subtle, it is almost scientific. It can be small and it can be large. Large amounts of pressure cause damage, cause change. Small amounts of pressure influence, encourage, and promote change. We take our time with the horse because we respect him. Our respect is shown through the careful use of pressure. We avoid damaging him with our pressure.

WE HAVE EARS IN OUR HANDS, OUR SEAT, OUR LEGS. WE NEED ONLY LISTEN WITH THEM.

The practice of reducing our pressure, we challenge ourselves to find the line between pressure and no pressure. We learn how to skirt that edge, to be finessed in our actions with the horse. Our actions become specific, subtle, sophisticated. We gain ultimate control over our actions, thereby increasing our ability to influence the horse with specificity.

Relative :

adjective
1. Not absolute; connected to or depending on something else.

preposition
1. Relating to, being relevant towards.

Even as we apply pressure to the horse, it changes. It cannot be stagnant or constant, it has to have it's own ebb and flow. In order to maintain consistency it must contain movement. To be still, we must move, and move in a way that is in harmony with the horse's movement. Whether this movement comes through us from the hands, the legs, the seat, our voice, our posture. Our movement is dependent upon the horse's movement.

This is the art of horsemanship. Contained in our movement and flow. When we attempt force or speed, inconsistencies or impatience, they are met with hesitations, they are met with interrupted movement.

Pressure is also all important in the subject of catching the horse, because our indiscriminate use of pressure causes the horse to run away, and then we often proceed to chase him. When we are conscious of the pressure we exude, it becomes simple to adjust it.

Practice the application of pressure at every moment, because the presence of pressure never ceases. It only increases and decreases, changes shape, direction, speed, and intention.

BEING A GREAT EQUESTRIAN IS ABOUT COMPREHENDING MORE IN A SINGLE LOOK OR PRESSURE IN THE HAND THAN ORDINARY EQUESTRIANS DO IN LONG INTERACTIONS OR THE MOST ELABORATE OF DISPLAYS.

IT IS HELD NOT IN COMPETITION WITH OTHERS, BUT WITH OURSELVES. IT IS HELD IN OUR MIND, OUR HANDS, OUR HEARTS. IT IS ABOUT OUR PASSION WITH THE HORSE.

NOTES

NOTES

NOTES

Stimulation which excites the horse to sporadic responses is neither helpful nor educational. We look for immediacy while missing subtlety. We expect our horse to listen, while we fail ourselves. Stimulation in itself is an art, a careful art. Too much and we kill what we sought. Too little and we fail to excite any response. Our job is to find the balance.

$\mathcal{S}$TIMULATION

Our overuse of pressure in any form results in frustration, confusion, anger, or fear in the horse. It may show up as hesitation or dulled responses just as easily as explosive energy or over-sensitivity. Our natural response to the resulting movement or action on the part of the horse is often to increase the pressure or stimulation we are using, or label the horse as being over-sensitive, high-strung, or out of control. According to the neurological system, we are working against nature.

> "WEAK STIMULI EXCITES PHYSIOLOGICAL ACTIVITY, MODERATELY STRONG ONES FAVOR IT, STRONG ONES RETARD IT, AND VERY STRONG ONES ARREST IT."
>
> ARDNT'S LAW OF NEUROLOGICAL STIMULATION

This is extremely important, because as the horse loses its responsiveness we must reduce our pressure and stimulation rather than increase it. We must listen to the horse's body, and support an increase in physiological activity.

NOTES

NOTES

Be careful. It is easy for us to forget harm done to us, but we will never forget the harm we do to our horse. It will haunt and hinder. Be careful, we must respect the safety and integrity of our horse.

ENTING

When we work with pressure, there is a threshold between touching and denting. Denting is when we move beyond touch and begin changing the integrity of the horse. In denting, we invade the horse – whether it is on a physical, mental, or emotional level.

We have lost the belief that the horse's opinion in regards to his well being is correct. Denting causes damage, whether it is physical, mental, or emotional; all are equally injurious to the horse. When our pressure is greater than the resistance it meets, we have begun denting the horse. Denting and force can be interchanged, although denting gives a visual as to the impact that force can have on the horse.

> WE ARE THE HORSE AND HE, US. WE ARE THE SAME.

Not only do we cause damage, we lose the horse's trust when we utilize denting. We must take careful practice to learn where the threshold between touching and denting exists. It is constantly changing shape and position, and in response we learn to move with it. We learn how to interact with the horse; train, ride and develop a relationship with him without causing damage, only influencing him subtly.

Denting can be created by the rider, or by the horse. We are responsible only for our part in denting. If the horse choses to move against us to such an extent as to dent himself, it is his own punishment. In the case of horses who have learned to habitually dent themselves as a means of coping with previously injurious training, we must be careful to clearly support a change in this habit through calm, consistent, and simple correction.

NOTES

NOTES

NOTES

Punishment must be done carefully. It hardens the heart, concentrates, and increases resistance. Punishment serves few purposes other than an outlet for our fears and angers.

RESISTANCE

Resistance exists in any situation where force is being utilized, one cannot exist without the other and their very definition relies on the opposite's presence.

Noun – force

1. Anything that is able to make a big change in a person or thing.
2. A physical quantity that denotes ability to push, pull, twist or accelerate a body and is measured in a unit dimensioned in mass x distance/time^2.
3. A group that aims to attack, control, or constrain.
4. The ability to attack, control, or constrain.
5. Either unlawful violence, as in a "forced entry", or lawful compulsion.

Verb – to force

1. **To exert violence, compulsion, or constraint upon or against a person or thing.**
2. To cause to occur, overcoming inertia or resistance.

Noun – resistance

1. The act of resisting, or the capacity to resist.
2. **A force that tends to oppose motion.**
3. Shortened form of electrical resistance.
4. An underground organization engaged in a struggle for liberation from forceful occupation.

We cannot escape the natural response of resistance when we are utilizing force. It is an unconscious response that is physical, mental, and emotional. We all have varying thresholds before our resistance comes into play. The horse is no different. Our use of force can often be unconscious as well, particularly before we become aware of the consequences that it can and does yield.

FORCE = RESISTANCE, RESISTANCE = FORCE

Our general view of resistance in regards to the horse has long been conditioned as being something we must change into submission and supplication. This endeavor is somehow intended to develop suppleness, as well as create a light, balanced, and responsive horse. The achievement of this kind of responsiveness through traditional methods of breaking a horse's resistance is like gaining a voiceless country through propaganda and military force, it is temporary. A country gained in this way will not remain this way, eventually resisting the force applied, just as the horse will resist the force being applied in time.

The amount of pressure we use with one horse is different than what we can use on another. No two horses are the same, they may be similar but never the same. As riders, our own interpretation of pressure will also vary. How we judge appropriate pressure is through our observation of the horse and his response to our actions.

THERE ARE FEW SIMPLE, ABSOLUTE ANSWERS OR ACTIONS IN HORSEMANSHIP.

NONE OF WHICH APPLY TO PRESSURE.

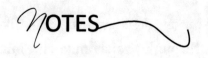

NOTES

NOTES

Actions are not general entities. Actions are specific. We do not seek or attain what we want in general. It is through our actions; which are specific, concrete, individualized, and unique that we achieve.

SPECIFICITY

No matter where we are in the training of the horse, we always approach it with as specific terms as possible. We look to where we are headed, using thoughts, words, and actions that support that achievement. Being vague in our goals does not leave room for achieving larger ones; it simply leaves room for not achieving the intended goal.

> **WHAT WE THINK, WE CREATE. WHEN WE THINK OF WHAT WE WANT, WE CREATE IT. WHEN WE THINK OF WHAT WE DO NOT WANT, WE CREATE IT.**
>
> **THINK POSITIVE. BE SPECIFIC.**

The use of negatives, like 'don't,' 'won't,' 'not,' do not process in our mind when we are chasing our dreams. To say that we "don't want the horse to buck" is like saying that we "want the horse to buck." We avoid using resistant terms to describe our goal. We describe what we want to happen, rather than what we want to avoid. In working this way, we know what and when we achieve our goal, as well as promoting fluidity and movement.

NOTES

NOTES

To reach high levels of equitation, we move beyond and past our ego and the dialogue of our mind. We let go of control, approval and judgement. We challenge ourselves to become more for the sake of the process. We give up challenges with the horse, with other riders. We stop fighting ourselves, we stop fighting life.

PRIDE, EGO & PERFECT ENDINGS

Through a long standing mantra, we are taught to always end on a good note. While this is good advice, it is often misinterpreted. More appropriately, we take the training of the horse only so far as to keep from exhausting the horse mentally, emotionally, or physically. Our work with the horse begins and ends while he is still capable of freely giving himself to our requests. What is more commonly seen however, is that riders use this saying to continue working their frustrated, confused or physically spent horse in an attempt to find the good note to end on.

DECIDE.

WHO REALLY WINS IF THE HORSE IS DEFEATED..?

The only good note is that which is held in the horse's opinion of us. When we sacrifice his respect, there is no 'good note' left to work towards. We keep our ego from abusing the horse's willingness to work to injury. Our pride is often working overtime when we put our ability to direct or control the horse in a specific manner over the horse's very well-being.

Other riders also see the driving force behind our actions. Decisions based on ego or pride rarely provide satisfaction. Much like a drug, we continue to desire more and more until our horse or ourselves break down as a result.

There is no shame in stopping on a bad note when we recognize our inability to use anything but force or excessive pressure, conflicting aids, or an expectation for the horse to perform beyond his present ability. It is only our pride that recognizes we have failed to 'win the battle,' when I wonder why we began fighting with our horse in the first place. Releasing our pressure in the moment of understanding we have used too much serves to repair and rebuild our relationship with the horse. When we stroke our pride instead, the horse and our relationship with him suffers.

> THE JOB OF EQUESTRIAN, IS THAT OF PROTECTING THE HORSE WHILE MAINTAINING AND DEVELOPING OUR RELATIONSHIP WITH HIM.
>
> NO 'SUCCESS' IS WORTH THE LIFE OF OURSELVES OR OUR HORSE. NEITHER IS THE RISK OF INJURY TO HIS MIND, BODY, HEART, OR SOUL.

NOTES

NOTES

NOTES

"A man who has committed a mistake and doesn't correct it, is committing another mistake."

Confucius

CORRECTION

Correction of self, or correction of the horse, must have a clear and distinct purpose. Even more, it must have a purpose which is not selfish or driven by fear, emotional weight, anger, or frustration. More simply put, correction which is not based upon the ego.

> **BY FEARLESSLY RIGHTING OUR WRONGS, WE GAIN THE FREEDOM OF EXPRESSION WITHOUT HESITATION.**

Correction can come as simply as words spoken to another person near you, written at just the right moment, or a hand on the shoulder that speaks more loudly than words ever could. With the horse, correction is often interchanged with clarification. Because the horse has little choice in the matter of a relationship with us, it must become an assumption in our own minds that any misunderstanding, evasion, diversion, distraction, reaction, etc., is through our own fault of lacking clarity in our request of the horse.

There are many ways of clarifying ourselves. We can repeat our request the same way as it was originally given, with the thought that perhaps the horse was not prepared or did not 'hear' it as we had given it. We can also give the request in a simpler form, with more or less emphasis, coming from a slightly different angle or direction, with more or less pressure, changing our position or posture, etc.

There is also the need to be observant of the horse in order to understand whether clarification is needed in the correction, of if the correction is simply taking a step back to a phase that the horse is prepared for and can perform. To change our expectation on the horse's preparedness for a movement or maneuver. To trust that the horse will give us feedback as to his readiness and fitness for a specific task.

The use of punishment should be kept extremely limited in the sense of interacting with the horse. Punishment does not encourage, but halts learning and development. It is an action that should be reserved solely for that which out of playfulness, exhuberance, or innocent inattentiveness comes actions which directly risk injury or death. Punishment to a horse who is acting out of nervousness, pain, fear, anger, frustration, or intentional inattentiveness will only exaggerate and increase the dangerous actions made by the horse.

Corrections made when the horse is in the place of fear,

nervousness, frustration, etc., should be those of redirection and reassurance. They must be actions that are calm and deliberate, confident and cool. They must reflect upon the horse that the handler feels no sense of danger in the situation and in this case present him as a leader, as setting the example. Redirecting the horse into actions that separate him from the anxiety helps, much as you would not begin analyzing the immense distance between yourself and the street down below while looking over the edge of a tall building, we likewise do not push the horse into a situation that he is reacting violently from.

NOTES

NOTES

Desire is not dependent upon the external. We can mistake desire for wanting things to make ourselves whole or greater or more special. Desire is self-serving and a never-ending pursuit. When our desires are on the level of working in the present moment, we become satisfied in that area. We stop craving the disappointing and unsavory sweets that promise to develop into a cavity, we grow and develop and are capable of greater development.

 What We Desire

In every facet of horsemanship, we seek to develop the horse through his gaits, directly or indirectly. We use different equipment, ride in different clothes, give different signals or aids, compete or ride for the pleasure. In the end, they are all different roads to the same Rome.

We gain influence and the capacity for developing a relationship through the horse's movement. This movement can refer to any direction, speed, posture, balance, or lack of. Whether we consider ourselves to be gaited, English, Western, Dressage, Eventing, or natural horsemanship riders, we all seek to develop the horse's gaits.

In all things, we expect only from the horse that which we are willing to do ourselves, including movement. If we are not fluid, the horse will not be fluid. Our imbalances support the horse's imbalances. Our rough and ragged responses support the horse's jerky movements. When we see what it is that we desire from the horse, we see what we desire from ourselves.

When we see what we wish to avoid with the horse, we likewise see what we wish to avoid with ourselves. There is no separation in our relationship. The horse is giving us direct feedback on the areas that we need to strengthen in ourselves as a rider, trainer, and person. This happens every time we interact.

Any desire outside of the horse's development is often ego-based. The reason for this is that its reward is dependent upon something that is more than what we have in the current moment. It is always reaching for satisfaction outside of the present.

We only live our lives in the present, every memory of the past, every thought to the future, we live them certainly but we can only live in the present. When our goals reach with a thought that we will be happy once we achieve this or that, we will reach that place and still be reaching for more. The satisfaction will not come, because it arrives in the present moment which our mind is no longer conscious of.

When we practice being conscious and aware in the moment we are living, satisfaction arrives at every moment of our life without the condition of some future experience, or a reliving of past events.

With horsemanship, the present moment is vital. The horse does not reach for the future or dwell in the past. The horse lives only for the moment it is presented with. It can certainly have developed habits or reactions based on a past experience, just the same as humans do. But the horse is not constantly reaching for something outside of himself.

Riding in the present moment is an experience much of euphoria and natural highs. It lifts the spirit, energizes the soul, and puts a smile on the face. It is the kind of experience that makes one want to spend every moment in the presence of the horse and relinquish all other responsibilities. It is what feeds a passionate equestrian.

NOTES

NOTES

We are predatory in nature, we see what we focus on. We often miss the forest for the trees. We must develop our focus, learn about our peripheral vision and seeing more, seeing outside of the past, outside of the assumptions. We must train our eyes to see what we are doing and cease focusing on where we have been or hope to go.

What we focus on, is what we create. When we focus on what it is that we do not want, we often get more of it with the horse, and in life. The riders who fear going fast struggle keeping their horse slow, and riders who hate going slow criticize their 'lazy' or unresponsive horse. We create the fast horse out of our resistance of speed, and we create the lazy, unresponsive horse in response to our constant need for speed and energy.

We serve as the horse's opposing pole in the quest for balance. When we stop resisting his pole, we are able to move closer to it, closer to balance and closer to harmony.

> "WHAT WE RESIST, PERSISTS."
>
> SONIA JOHNSON

A horse can and will learn intelligently to be light, balanced and responsive without any encounter with resistance, only when the rider achieves communication that uses no force or resistance themselves. Our aim is avoiding the creation of a submissive horse, because to submit means that there was resistance in the first place and resistance cannot exist without the presence of force.

> **FOCUSING ON FEARS MAKES THEM GROW.**
>
> **FOCUSING ON IMMEDIATE ACTIONS MAKES FEARS SHRINK.**

When we want something from the horse that he is not offering, the continuation to dwell on the diversion he is giving us fails to achieve a solution. Instead we must focus specifically on the action we want to replace the diversion with. We think and act in a manner that is consistent with achieving something. If we do not know what it is we want, we cannot take the steps necessary to reach the goal.

We often fall into the thinking somewhere between negative and positive, what I like to call the 'I'm Fine Zone.' We use vague and non-descriptive terms rather than anything specific, anything tangible. What does it mean to be 'fine'?

The same goes for riding and training our horse. We avoid focusing on the negative, "Don't buck!" and give our thoughts and actions positive and achievable focus, "Calm, balanced, and forward canter departure." Our negative thoughts are the means for our resistance of what the horse is giving us, of what we are not achieving.

Our resistance is a sign of lost movement, while movement is the very thing we are attempting to gain from the horse. Resistance contains little consistency other than its own existence. This is where we lose our fluidity, our tact, our creativity. You cannot paint a portrait if you focus on all of the things you don't want it to look like.

There are two important factors involved in focus, that which is natural to the predator (humans), and that which is natural to the prey (horses).

For the predatory animal to be successful in living, it must concentrate on one item in its consciousness and focus all of its energy in that direction excluding all else that could distract it. That is how the predator catches its prey, its dinner, its objectives in life deemed necessary to survival.

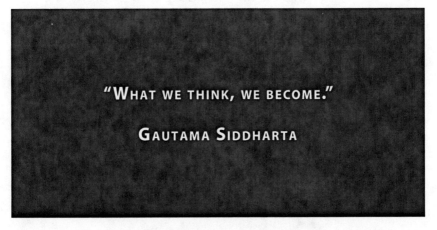

"WHAT WE THINK, WE BECOME."

GAUTAMA SIDDHARTA

On the opposite end of the spectrum, is the prey animal, the horse, whose whole existence relies upon its ability to observe the big picture and all of the details of its surroundings without ever giving enough time concentrating on any single object that it misses another detail which could be a danger. The horse's attention touches from one place to the next to the next continuously; it may pause at times to investigate potential danger, and then resume the scan.

Both predator and prey base their attention on the need to survive, one for food and the other from becoming food. When we interact as predatory animals with a prey animal, it is important to seek our eternally dynamic balance. When we stop resisting the horse, we find that we begin to become entrained with him. We come more in sync with his characteristics and vice versa him with ours. This serves us well, and communication becomes clearer and harmonized.

In order to find this balance we must practice the ability to de-focus our attention. To lose sight of the detail in a singular object and scan the horizon so to speak. To hear our surroundings - the multiplicity of them, and to process it simultaneously. This, requires practice.

Likewise, in our work with the horse we wish to carefully draw his attention closer and closer to a single object - us. In order to do that we must first move closer and closer to his means of attention, that is through consistent inconsistency. Stimulation that is consistent, but constantly changing in order to incite the horse's natural response to bring attention to the changes surrounding him.

There is a secondary purpose that focus fulfills as well that is vital; that of observation and becoming a witness. To observe the trip, the journey, and appreciate it as much or more than the destination. Because to miss the journey is to only taste a drop of the life one is living.

NOTES

NOTES

Work only for yourself. How can anyone else know what gives us true joy and happiness better than ourselves? They cannot, and if on the road to living your happiness you should cross paths with someone, great. If not, do not concern yourself, do not dwell on that expectation. Our happiness will guide us in the right direction.

XPECTATIONS

The horse can come to expect certain habits or actions from us, just the same as we of them. Our expectations from the horse are precisely that which we give to him. When we use force to ask for a movement, we can expect him to use force in response. This force can be compromised compliance or direct resistance, often it is both. When we use lightness and consistency in asking for a movement, we likewise expect a light and consistent response.

Expectations are far more powerful than we often give them credit for. An expectation held in our mind can be responsible for helping create either a strong relationship with the horse, or a relationship based on difficulty and continuous power struggles. Expectations can keep us locked into habitual patterns with a horse, and they can also be used to break free from those patterns. When we focus our expectations on the horse, it is important to note that we can only expect from the horse what we are capable of ourselves in that moment. Also, we can only expect from our horse what we would be capable of in his position at that moment. We remember our compassion, our ability to see ourselves being the same as the horse.

NOTES

NOTES

We can be responsible only for ourselves and it is in our attempt to be responsible for the horse or others around us that confusion and difficulty ensue.

CENTER, CENTER... CENTER

We experience times when our horse seems completely calm at a very distracting event or absolutely frazzled in the calmest surroundings. This is not uncommon in the least, and is all too often dismissed as being caused by the horse's mental or emotional roller coasters. This seemingly logical explanation does not do the horse, or ourselves, justice.

What we recognize in the horse, is a reflection of our own mental or emotional state or presence. If the horse is distracted, why are we distracted by the horse's distracted actions? If the horse is afraid of the unknown or invisible, where are we fearful ourselves? When the horse gives us these responses it is when we react to them, giving them stories or excuses, that we know they are a part of what we are experiencing in other areas of our own lives. When the horse gives us these responses and we are centered, they have no strength, simply becoming part of the training path.

When interacting with the horse, we become his herd. We either support or disarm his reactions.

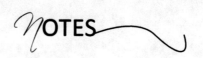

NOTES

NOTES

Often the simplest of answers are the most correct. Often the simplest of answers are the most complicated. Often the simplest of answers are the most difficult to find the question needed to elicit it.

CLEAR & SIMPLE

The way in which we interact with the horse, is done on the simplest plane possible. Even the most complicated of expectations can be achieved through the use of simple means. Considerable confusion in riders involves their use and understanding of complicated, complex, and oppositional aids. It is no wonder that as a result horses are confused as well.

> WE COMPLICATE THAT WHICH WE DO NOT FULLY UNDERSTAND. IT GIVES US THE FEELING OF IMPORTANCE, OF KNOWLEDGE.

By using several aids together, or in a complex arrangement, we feel that we are doing something important. We are simply keeping ourselves busy with all of this activity. It is amazingly difficult to do little or nothing, compared to constant movement and action.

> ### CONFIDENT KNOWLEDGE REQUIRES NO IMPORTANCE.
>
> ### IT REQUIRES SIMPLE.

Already at our disposal are an unlimited number of movements and responses achievable from the horse with the use of a single aid, rendering the use of several aids together unnecessary. In consideration, that with a single aid you have an infinite number of variations involved through the components of pressure, direction, duration, consistency, and movement, we are left with no use for additional aids. We also have influence based upon the gait we work at, speed involved, the horse's posture, balance, and bend, as well as our own position and posture in or out of the saddle.

> ### SIMPLE, DOES NOT MEAN EASY.

As we progress we can choose to attempt the use of combined aids to add refinement to our aids and movements, or we can choose to continue refining the use of singular aids. Both endeavors have potentially positive results. No matter our focus, the singular or combined use of the aids changes that of the other. We work to avoid becoming reliant upon either, with the ability to utilize both in an equally skilled manner.

In our use of combined aids, we must continue to keep our communication simple. We do not confuse or conflict our aids. When we meet resistance or confusion with the horse, we correct it by simplifying our aids even further. We never work a horse through confusion with multiple aids apart from the "combined effect."

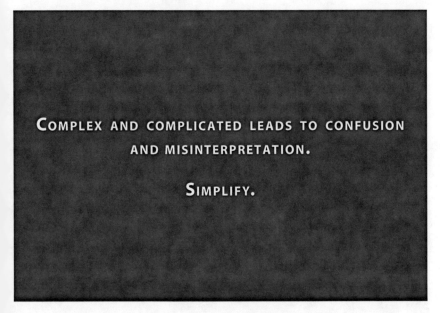

COMPLEX AND COMPLICATED LEADS TO CONFUSION
AND MISINTERPRETATION.

SIMPLIFY.

NOTES

Notes

Action proves more effective than opposition. To oppose is to be mindful of what we wish to avoid. To act is to grab hold of what we want and sail on the wind with it!

OPPOSITION

We are taught in a traditional manner that in order to balance out the overuse of one aid, we use an opposing aid. We function as though we are driving a car and have to correct the overuse of the steering wheel. Throughout our education, we aim to learn that instead of relying on correction we become masters of using the aids with such precision that correction is not necessary.

> **OPPOSITION RUINS INSPIRATION.**
>
> **INSPIRATION NURTURES OUR GROWTH AS RIDERS.**
>
> **WE DO NOT OPPOSE OUR OWN LEARNING.**

Our initial education leads us to use aids expecting the complete opposite of the natural reaction they inspire in the horse. In the simplification of our aids and communication with the horse, we are maximizing the probability of success by using as few unnatural conditioned responses from the horse as possible.

The traditional use of the legs is an exemplary show of this initial education. Having been taught to move the horse forward by applying more pressure with our legs the faster we wish the horse to go forwards, we set the stage for creating horses which buck when first started under saddle. The horse's natural response to leg pressure is to contract, not expand, the abdominal muscles. We miss the fine understanding that it is with the release of leg pressure that we inspire forward movement. Necessarily, there must be pressure of some amount applied, but more important than the amount of pressure is the emphasis in the release.

> **WHEN WE RELY ON STRENGTH TO DO WHAT WE HAVE NOT LEARNED TO FINESSE, WE DO SO WITH OPPOSITION.**

The same is true of the commonly taught aids and cues, being illogical to the horse and only conditionally understood by us. We apply pressure to the horse's chest to ask him to move backwards or stop, when it is his natural instinct to move into pressure. We pull back on the reins to stop, when the horse's natural instinct is to move into pressure. We increase pressure when there is no response, when no response is often a sign of already too much pressure being applied.

Opposition requires longer to successfully train the horse than do aids and actions which are naturally supported by the horse's instincts.

NOTES

NOTES

Like a beautiful song is ruined by a separated chord, so is the relationship between horse and rider by a separated perspective. All of our work with the horse is in someway directed at closing the gap that separates us. Our mind must also follow this belief.

We look at the horse as being ourselves. We consider his feelings and safety throughout riding and training, whether our our riding simply fun, art or competitive. When he suffers, so do we. He is our mirror and we are his. Where we struggle or excel in other areas of our life has an impact on our relationship with the horse. Where we struggle or excel with our horse likewise impacts other areas of our life.

> **HARMONY IS THE COMBINED SKILL OF EVERY ELEMENT.**
>
> **SEPARATION SERVES TO DISRUPT HARMONY.**

For this reason, and all the more, what we desire in the horse we have to seek in ourselves. What we expect in the horse we first expect in ourselves. We may certainly purchase a horse which has the quality we are seeking, but if we do not have it the horse begins to lose that quality. He takes on our qualities, and we take on his, as we are drawn to a balance between both ourselves and the horse.

NOTES

NOTES

To find the center, we have to know the ends. To find the balance we have to know both sides of imbalance. This is how we refine our balance, to know our limitations and have intimacy with the aids and cues we use with the horse.

BBALANCE

Coupled with harmony, balance is an important element involved in training the horse. Balance plays a part in creating the harmony we seek, and it is a factor in determining the proper use of any aids or cues. Balance has two extremes, two opposing ends of an action, movement or energy. These extremes give us a guiding map to where the center is located, also known as balance.

> **BALANCE IS THE RESULT OF TWO EQUAL AND OPPOSING IMBALANCES.**

Balance exists with the presence of two equally distant extremes. Likewise, balance is experienced with the full exploration of those two extremes. Just as a teeter totter with only one rider finds only one extreme, the same can be said of the aids and cues we use with the horse. To know what hot is, we must first know what is cold and vice versa. To know where balance lies when we ride with too much pressure on the reins, we have to explore the extreme of too little pressure. Likewise, when we are too light and giving with the reins we have to explore the polar extreme of the rein aids, using more pressure than we are comfortable with. It is this exploration of the extremes that enables our intelligent understanding in the achievement of balance.

This exploration of extremes applies to both our education and that of our horse. We explore the extremes of our own actions, and we likewise teach the horse that he too has extremes of his own. This teaches the horse how to be intelligently balanced, eliminating the need for oppositional aids and cues.

We avoid the safe haven of belief that we have achieved all the skill possible in understanding and achieving balance. Balance changes based on factors outside of ourselves and therefore, outside of our control. To know when we have achieved balance we need only look at the horse for proof.

Balance exists on many levels. It is physical, mental, and emotional. Balance is involved in the speed, strength, direction, and movement; or intention of our actions, words, touch, or thoughts. Balance is involved in every aspect of our lives.

In the education of the horse, we explore the extremes of bend, balance, posture, and speed. We teach the horse fast and slow gaits, high and low posture, on the forehand and on the haunches, left or right bend. To achieve straight we learn both left and right. To be balanced we achieve too much and too little. The understanding of these extremes is what brings consistency to the balance we desire.

The same expectation is on the part of the rider. We learn to ride leaning too far forwards and backwards to understand where the middle ground is. We learn to have hands too high and too low to know where the middle is. We seek the ability to sit the trot too slowly and too quickly to find the balance that equalizes the horse's bounce.

KEEP WORKING AT SOMETHING LONG ENOUGH AND YOU WILL FIND YOURSELF AT THE BEGINNING. IF YOU MOVE FASTER AND FASTER, YOU WILL EVENTUALLY FIND YOURSELF MOVING SLOWLY. MOVE SLOWER AND SLOWER AND YOU WILL FIND SPEED.

We avoid the use of on and off switches, and confusing them with balance. On and off switches lack a sliding scale. Our aim is to use dimmers in all we do and expect from the horse, having an unlimited number of variations in their response. The presence of yes or no, on or off, in or out, forward or backwards, up or down, black or white are all on and off switches. As riders and trainers, we are made up of grey shades, the same as the horse.

Before we can know what is right, we must know what is wrong. We cannot appreciate ease until we've experienced difficulty. The same is true of riding. To know one extreme fully we first learn the opposite. We seek balance in all we do with the horse, but to know balance is to be experienced in both ends of imbalance.

NOTES

NOTES

NOTES

Equitation is a dance. It is a dance with equal partners, we lead and are led, the horse leads and is led. We change places as it is appropriate. To hold a constant position is to utilize force, resistance, and over-stimulation. There is no constant in equitation, rather it is dynamic. It is constantly dynamic.

RELATIONSHIP HIERARCHY

The horse – human relationship is capable of balance, just as any other interaction. When our communication is clear and simple, the use of leader and follower mentality is unnecessary. A dominant – submissive relationship with the horse is less desirable. When our actions are fair and balanced, the horse's responses will be the same. Just like our experience with the extremes of balance, when we seek to make the horse submissive, we meet horses who fight for the opposite extreme or those who have their resistance broken and finally follow obediently. Anytime the horse is caused to make a decision to become dominant or submissive in the relationship, force has been implemented.

We seek to make the horse our equal in every step of the relationship. There are certainly times when they will look to us for guidance in a situation that is unfamiliar or frightening, in return we give our respect by returning their ability as an equal. When we consider being dominant in the relationship with the horse, it means that we have committed ourselves to the thought that we know what is right for the horse more than he does himself. This mind-set also leads us to believe that in some way we are better, smarter, faster, or more skilled than the horse. We do not invest our time with the thought that our horse is less than we are.

Again, the ego comes into play in the case of a leader – follower relationship with the horse. The ego wants to believe that we are the leader, that we have to be the leader all the time. Or, perhaps the ego wants to be a follower, and so gives the horse all grounds to walk upon him, with the idea that the horse is leading them. Being flexible in the role of leader – follower as needed is the sign of relinquishing the ego.

NOTES

NOTES

NOTES

Confidence is born out of self trust. When we trust ourselves there is no hesitation in our decisions, answers, actions. We move instinctually, naturally, fluidly. Without trust there can be no harmony, there is too much thought, too much questioning. Harmony is our trusting instincts in motion.

TRUST

An elemental quality in any relationship is that of trust. Without the potential for trust our relationship with the horse becomes one of slave and master, prisoner and guard. Trust is what lays the foundation for interaction with the horse on a level that may be at times difficult to fully digest. Trust is what makes an ordinary juggling team an extraordinary one as they throw chain saws, flaming torches and deadly knives towards one another at lightning speed.

> **TRUST EVERY MISTAKE IS PERFECT, NECESSARY.**

Trust is a quality that is easily lost, and difficult to obtain. It is one of those intangible qualities, which we search for but cannot hold in our hand or hang on the wall. We take every precaution in keeping our horse's trust, including the avoidance of placing the horse in any situation where that trust could be broken. We avoid putting the horse in any position that could knowingly jeopardize his life, we avoid causing him pain or discomfort, and we avoid the use and reliance on equipment or gimmicks to control or constrain him. We do everything in our power to remove the element of ownership from the relationship.

Part of trust is belief in the horse's reasons for an action or behavior, rather than attempting to dismiss him as having no cause or just reason. We trust that when the horse is in pain, that he will tell us and have good reason to do so. We trust that when the horse is afraid for his life, that he has good reason to be. This kind of trust and equality is vital for a strong relationship with the horse. When we fail to trust his ability to keep himself safe or take care of himself, it is like saying that he is not capable of living without us, the perfect breeding grounds for discontent.

TRUST BEGINS IN OURSELVES. WHEN WE LACK TRUST IN OURSELVES IT OFTEN APPEARS AS MISTRUST IN OUR HORSE AND OTHER RIDERS. TO BUILD TRUST IN OTHERS WE MUST FIRST HAVE TRUST IN OURSELVES.

In the end, we want trust, not dependence. The use or threat of pain, hunger, injury, fear, or death to achieve our goals is not made available in our training. There is never an opportunity in which deprivation of his basic needs is appropriate.

NOTES

NOTES

We have control until we do not. We cannot lose control, to lose it would assume that we had it to begin with. What we mistake for control is knowing. How we find knowing is by listening, being aware. Awareness leads to knowing, which is the real form of control.

Controlling Our Control

A harmonious relationship requires no control, it simply is what it is in that moment, with both participants in balance with the other. Where we face issues with control is when we seek it. If we do not introduce the idea of control to the horse, we can never be without and there is no need for it. Control is something that is unachievable without force. If we are using force, the horse will present resistance, encouraging increased force to create submission. This is how the breakdown begins.

> CONTROL: A BEAUTIFUL MYTH PROMISING MANY THINGS UNFULFILLED.

Control is something which is intangible. No matter our efforts to control our horse, ourselves, or the elements of our life, it is all a momentary figment of our imagination. Anyone who has experienced a catastrophic event such as a hurricane or tornado, sudden illness, death in the family, etc., have a keener sense of this. That no matter how we prepare or attempt to control the direction in which our lives turn, there are always variables that we cannot predict and therefore cannot influence, leaving us truly without control.

Control is only ours until we no longer have control. It is that magical idea that when life is traveling the enjoyable and carefree path that we have control, and when it is spinning faster than we would like we have lost control. It is only a thought, an idea, a theory. Inevitably, when we attempt control it only moves further away from us, we chase the imaginary and unachievable.

In many ways, our relationship with the horse balances on the edge of desiring control. We seek to have control over the horse, and the horse often seeks control over the situations he is put into. Our motivation for this control is based on the same principle of the horse's – that of protecting ourselves. We begin to think that if we have control, we will be safe. The horse also thinks the same thoughts, if they have control they will be saved from injury or death from this predatory 'partner.'

AVOID THE DESTRUCTIVE NATURE OF 'CONTROL,' THAT OF CREATING HESITATION AND STOPPING FLUIDITY.

When we do not look for control, the horse follows suit. The horse's own desire for control recedes because he mimics us. This is easier said than done, because it is built into our core just as it is with the horse. We fight against our own natural instinct, and the key is to find this loss of control without the fight element. Only then is it truly loss of control, because when we fight we are still attempting control.

Part of seeking control is a mind reaching for the future, for the 'what if' that haunts it. The mind that is functioning in the present moment is not plagued with the need for control, because outside of the here and now there is nothing else. Nothing to be controlled.

NOTES

NOTES

Difficulty is the opportunity for further growth. Without difficulty we could not hope to achieve the heights possible in it's presence. A grand opportunity for further growth and development.

$\mathcal{D}$IFFICULTY

There are times, inevitably, that we experience difficulty with our horse. Difficulty can put a halt on our plans for continuous improvement and development of the horse; it can also be extremely frustrating as we attempt to find a solution that may not seem to exist. Maybe our horse is continuously tossing his head, rushing into the bit, spooking at the invisible monster in the corner, won't stand still for mounting, or offers a buck at every canter depart.

> **NOTHING WORTH PURSUING IS ENTIRELY FREE FROM DIFFICULTIES.**

As with the other lessons we teach the horse, it is through our observational skills that we can find the answer our horse is giving to us. In every case of difficulty, there is a reason. Horses do not go to the trouble of any action or movement that takes energy without a reason behind it. When we trust in the thought that the horse always has a good reason for his actions it takes away the tendency of anger at the horse's lack of compliance with our desires.

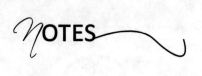

NOTES

NOTES

A working meditation of sorts, we surrender our thoughts on everything outside of the now, outside of our work with the horse. This form of concentration, of awareness, allows us to find the intricacies involved in equitation.

Full Commitment

Our full commitment to whatever we do with the horse is our way of showing the horse that he is all important. If we want his respect, we must give it in return and this includes all of our attention. When we ask for a movement, we commit all of our energy to supporting that. When we ask for the horse's undivided attention, we likewise give him ours by eliminating all of our distractions.

> **OUR MIND FUNCTIONS IN THE MOMENT BEST. LET GO OF WHAT IS NOT IN THE PRESENT, EMBRACE WHAT YOU HAVE IN YOUR HANDS.**

When we head to the arena, we must leave the rest of our world behind us. When we are facing stress at work or with a family member, it is all too easy to take it with us to the barn. Many times as riders, that is exactly what we use the horse's company for – to help relieve our stress. The horse, often considered a beast of burden, should not be used as a dumping ground for our inconsistencies any more than any other person around us.

WE MIMIC OUR HORSE, HE MIMICS US.

Our relationship with the horse will inevitably bring out feelings and emotions in us that we face with other people, and by full commitment to the horse I mean that our intentions are to work through those issues rather than attempting to hide or ignore them. Like a pressure cooker, these hidden problems do not stay hidden for long. Maybe we've had a great streak of excellent rides, only to find that every 4 or 5 rides we have one just absolutely rotten ride when the horse absolutely refuses to do anything we ask for. This is not the horse's issue, this is our own. When we allow our stresses to build up, they eventually explode. When we deal with them as they occur, we allow no time for the build up and our interactions with the horse level to consistency.

TO HAVE A HORSE IN THE MOMENT, WE MUST BE LIKE-WISE. TO HAVE A HORSE FOCUSED ON THE NOW, WE SET THE EXAMPLE FIRST.

NOTES

NOTES

NOTES

All things are a possibility until they are not, even those yet undreamed.

ENDLESS POSSIBILITIES

When we work and train our horses, it helps to keep the thought in mind that anything is possible. Possibilities do not require a full understanding of how they are achieved in order to achieve them. If that was true we would have never invented the wheel. Horses are amazing creatures, just as we are, and their limitations are not as narrow as we would like to believe or be led to believe at times.

> IN THE BEGINNING WE THINK THE MOST BASIC OF TASKS DIFFICULT OR IMPOSSIBLE. THE CHALLENGES SEEM TOO GREAT. THEN WE MASTER THEM AND THEY ARE SIMPLE. THIS NEVER CHANGES, THEY SIMPLY TAKE ON NEW SHAPES. EVEN THE MOST ACCOMPLISHED HAVE NEW POSSIBILITIES IN THEIR REACH.

As we witness events or actions, or are involved in things that make us sit back and wonder, we have been privy to the miracle of invention. We have been included in something so amazing that our mind previously had not been able to conceptualize it. We see these amazing things every day, though we may not always be fully conscious of them until they show up in in such an obvious form that we cannot ignore their presence.

The horse who has been trained beyond grand prix dressage, despite his lack-luster pedigree and homely conformation or none-too-attractive movement, only to show he shines just as brightly as the rest with the right rider relationship. Or the horse who has overcome the impossible to not just live an average life, but one which the most carefully brought up horses never reached. We've witnessed the same in people as well.

As riders, we all have equal footing, just the road that differs. We all experience a trip here or there, and a short-cut that proves to be anything but short. We get stuck, we get discouraged, we wonder if this is really right for us. On the same stroke of luck, we also find encouragement, excitement, joy, and heavenly happiness, often at times least expected.

IF YOU CAN IMAGINE IT, YOU CAN ACHIEVE IT.

Those with great talents also have great weaknesses, it is only our perception which classifies them as good or bad.

We sometimes shy away from attempting new or unusual movements, actions, or methods for fear of criticism, judgment, or failure. I say it's time to think like Thomas Jefferson and create our own light bulb.

NOTES

NOTES

Order works well with machines. Order is reliably consistent with tangibly inanimate objects. The horse is not subject to these rules, he changes, he feels, he grows.

TRAINING ORDER

There are categorized and highly detailed lists of how training is intended to progress, from the basics to the advanced. At times these may seem like rules, but they could be interpreted as guidelines instead.

ORDER SUCCEEDS ONLY IN A CIRCULAR FASHION. WHEN WE BASE IT ON A LINEAR FORM THERE IS SEPARATION FROM GROWTH. THE TRAINING NEVER ENDS, THE FIRST STEP CONTINUES TO THE LAST STEP, WE REPEAT CONTINUALLY THROUGHOUT TRAINING AND RIDING, THROUGHOUT LEARNING AND TEACHING.

In the training of the horse, the only order of progression that matters is that which is understood by the horse. This is an order that cannot be described in any general scheme.

Each horse has to be approached as an individual, with the time, approach, and method personalized in each case.

Where we run into road blocks is when we attempt to train all horses using the same order, when we lose our flexibility and fluidity. We become mechanized, the very thing we wish to avoid with the horse. We like to think that the instructions suited to guide us in the training of all horses will help shorten the time needed to take the horse from baby to advanced competitor, when it is often these very guidelines that in their aim to help, end up hindering our goal.

ORDER MUST CHANGE AND FLOW, JUST AS THE HORSE DOES. OUR TRAINING FOLLOWS AFTER THE HORSE, TAKES INPUT FROM THE HORSE AND CHANGES AS A RESULT. ALL THINGS ARE DONE APPROPRIATELY FOR THE HORSE, THAT IS WHEN IT MAKES THE MOST SENSE.

Our training order is in a constant state of flux, while it may have been appropriate to work on a specific area with the horse yesterday, today is a whole new day and with it may come different variables that affect how we should approach the horse. The horse which excelled when taught leading, then lunging, and then riding, is not the same horse who excels when taught lunging, then grooming, then leading, then riding.

NOTES

NOTES

We summarize in words, that which we cannot summarize in communication with the horse. We conflict - words with communication.

UMMARY

We never evolve in a linear fashion, that is A to Z with A being the beginning and Z the end. Instead, we circle around continuously, only to cover the same topic, idea, theory, thought, action, movement, over and over again. While we may develop a deeper understanding or new level to these different factors, we never learn them completely, we never find an end.

> **WE ARE PATIENT. PATIENCE LENDS ITSELF TO DISCOVERY. DISCOVERY LEADS TO GREATER UNDERSTANDING AND DEPTHS UNREACHABLE WITHOUT PATIENCE.**

It is this thinking that allows us to take the horse's training to a higher level. The way we work the horse in the beginning of his training is the same as we work him at the end. The way we work our horse at the end of his training is the same way we work at the beginning. While we may develop more refinement, subtleties, and skill there is always room for improvement. We are always at the beginning and always at the end. There is nothing we do in the beginning that cannot be considered finished, and there is nothing we finish that cannot be considered just a beginning.

We are the same as our horses; our own development is also circular. We continuously revisit the same skills, actions, movements, thoughts, feelings, emotions. It is easy to believe that there is a start and a finish, and it is also easy to be discouraged when we never find that finish. We do not find it because it does not exist. We can be out of touch with a particular area that we believe we have finished for some time, only to have it walk through the door when least expected. We never finish, we only continue to learn, grow, change, develop, and understand. We do this for our entire lives.

KEEP MOVING, EVEN MOVEMENT BACKWARDS IS MOVEMENT IN THE RIGHT DIRECTION. WHEN WE STOP WE BEGIN TO WITHER AND DIE, WE LOSE WHAT WE HAVE LEARNED. MOVE IN ANY WAY YOU CAN.

PHYSICALLY, MENTALLY, EMOTIONALLY.

This book addresses the very thought, it is not a book to read once and set down unless you want to. Every book holds new possibilities and meanings every time you read it, the content is not linear. To pick up a book and read it in a sad mood can bring attention to certain words and detail that is not present when you are in a happy mood.

What we become aware of, we see more of. We often do not see that which we are unaware of or do not understand. It is easy to be clouded from the prevalence of mild to moderate lameness until we begin to trim hooves. It is easy not to see the tension held in the horse whose nose band is tightly fitted to hold his mouth shut until we learn about the ramifications of such an action.

When we begin to find awareness in these areas, it is easy to begin championing every cause that seems unjust. It is also easy to become overwhelmed by the powerful emotions and thoughts that come to mind. This is the part where we must remain motivated to learn, get hungry for knowledge and skill. Pursue our passion, and do everything in our power to chase our dreams. Passionate people are those who change the world. They are the ones who seem to attract people simply by stepping into the room, without having to say a word, because the energy involved in pursuing our passion is so strong we find it overflowing.

This book is not about giving the answers. It is about giving guidelines, of which it is my honest hope that they inspire us to dig for more. Learn from every resource around us, the horse, other riders and trainers, even family members and children give us insights into how to communicate and interact with the horse. If we ever wonder about a new communication method, try it out on a friend or relative first and see what our results are, they will often mimic that of the horse.

"*THE TRUTH IS THAT OUR FINEST MOMENTS ARE MOST LIKELY TO OCCUR WHEN WE ARE FEELING DEEPLY UNCOMFORTABLE, UNHAPPY, OR UNFULFILLED. FOR IT IS ONLY IN SUCH MOMENTS, PROPELLED BY OUR DISCOMFORT, THAT WE ARE LIKELY TO STEP OUT OF OUR RUTS AND START SEARCHING FOR DIFFERENT WAYS OR TRUER ANSWERS.*"

M. SCOTT PECK

This book was written for all of the injustices witnessed, defended or participated in with regard to the horses and people in life. It is my part to make a difference, to show my passion, to pass on what I have learned in an effort to show that there are ways of achieving a profound level of horsemanship, beyond anything comprensible in the mind. This book is also for the wonderful group of horses that I have the pleasure of working with and for all that they have given me in the way of feedback, lessons, and compassion. In particular: Scout who allowed me to learn most of my mistakes with and still be eager to relearn what I have corrected in my methods; Ceylon, the most stubborn and difficult horse I have had to work with from the day she was born and as a result taught me most importantly the lesson of a present mind, proving to be the best horse I could ever ask for.

NOTES

NOTES

NOTES

NOTES

NOTES

CPSIA information can be obtained at www.ICGtesting.com
Printed in the USA
LVOW122122010213

318253LV00001B/198/P